"LIL BROTHERS, HEAR ME OUT!"

Laura Simmons

Table of Contents

"Stay true to yourself and be your own man."

--Horace--

Wisdom

Stay focused on what you want out of life. Only you can control your own destiny.

Never hesitate to manifest your own dreams into reality.

Jason
Tattoo Artist/ Illustrator/ Rapper

<u>Never Doubt A Woman</u>

First, I want to say to you my Lil Brothers, if you are reading this page I must have gotten your attention I know you are probably saying to yourself what could this woman possible have to say to us? Well hear me out I am a daughter to a father, a sister to several brothers, a wife to a husband, a mother to a son, an aunt to several nephews, a niece to several uncles, and so on…My point is I know a whole lot of men that were once Lil brothers just like you. Never doubt a woman as she created by the rib of a man. Although Man was first, it was women who give birth. We are capable of so many things…. but I'm not here to talk about women, I'm here to tell you what my Brothers shared with me and I in turn want to share that wisdom with you, Lil brothers who are truly in this struggle. Do I have all the answers? No, I don't but does anyone? No not at all. Will I pretend to know all the answers? No, but I'm going to tell you all what I do know if you are willing to hear me out.

Laura Simmons
Author/Motivational Speaker

<u>Love You First</u>

First, I want to start by telling my Lil Brothers to love you first and foremost. Then I want to say, "You are uniquely handsome in your own way", so applaud yourselves. It's okay to look different and be different that's what make you unique in your own special way. Big muscles, little muscles and no muscles now repeat after me: I am unique, muscles doesn't define me. Light skin, dark skin now repeat after me: I am still unique, skin tone doesn't define me. Thin or thick repeat after me: I am who I am supposed to be. I am unique. Weight doesn't define me.

Repeat after me: I can run the world because I am unique!

"You must always be comfortable in your own skin!!"
--Lee Robinson--

<u>Being Molded Into Young Men</u>

Lil Brothers, you are still learning yourself and people will use that to persuade you to do anything if you allow them that kind of control over you. They will tell you whatever they think you want to hear to get you. That's why it's vital for you to listen to your parents closely so they can mold you and get you ready for the world. Be careful about letting irrelevant people control and shape who you are becoming.

"They should obey their parents, fear God and serve him."
--Prophet Fitzroy Green--

<u>Be Careful About Thinking Everyone Is Your Friend</u>

Lil Brothers, be conscious of people you surround yourself with because some people desire to use you for their own practical purposes. People tend to dismiss you when there is no use for you anymore. This is how some will choose to treat you. Then, there are the people that want to be you, but always trying to make you second guess yourself.

If, and when you run into these types of people keep this in mind, the decision you make now can destroy you later. Just because you can doesn't mean you should. Remember to take a step back and look in the mirror. If you like what you see, don't worry about what someone else thinks of you. Be careful of the people that are just in your life for the ride because those people will try to use your successes or fails against you. This is why it is very important that you do not share all your thoughts and dreams with everyone.

Oh, and believe me my Lil Brothers, I'm not slinging mud or shade on any of the other brothers, but what I do know is that every shoe doesn't fit everyone: while some shoes were designed to fit certain feet, it can be the same way with people, some of us were not designed to gel together. Then there are those of us who will connect like two peas in a pod, because that's just life.

As I think back on life, I can recall my parents and what some of you call "the old heads" used to say "Keep living because it's a lot you will learn about people and life." It doesn't matter what nationality, gender or age, people will be people.

"Always ask questions, be a good listener surround yourself with quality people, listen to the voice of experience and always treat people the way you want to be treated."
--Tim Grant--

<u>Fitting In</u>

Lil Brothers, Remember you have a choice in life, so choose wisely. I remember watching my brothers go through their many changes between 13 to 18 years of age. They were trying to find themselves as they went through different changes in their appearance and voice. Oh my!! My brothers were really going through it. They dealt with inner city youth issues stemming from gang bangers to girlfriends! OMG! They were trying to figure out where they fit in with the crowd and yes that's normal, but it was not easy for them at all. Nevertheless, they stayed strong because they had strong men around them, from Dad, uncles, friends' fathers and men on the corners. That's when the community' was their family too.

No we weren't all meant to look alike or be the same size or all to be athletic.

Growing up, my brothers went through it all, so many changes, but guess what? For the most part, they are still standing tall because they took life by the hand and created their own circle or crowd that fit their criteria. I definitely know being a kid isn't easy. And guess what-being an adult isn't either.

"Set goals in life for yourself and develop self-discipline to stay the course and overcome your obstacles."

--David--

<u>Trust</u>

Trusting everyone you meet should be a hard thing to do. This brings me back to when my mom use to tell my brothers everyone isn't your friend. I remember a time when one of my brother's got into a lot of trouble with some of the boys from my old neighborhood. I recall hearing my use the saying: Birds of a feather flock together (meaning people that act a like usually hang together.) I remember she also told us that it's easy as heck to get into trouble but it's hard as hell to get out of trouble.

"You have the choice to choose wisely so trust your inner self."
--Author/Motivational Speaker Laura Simmons--

<u>Stay The Course</u>

Lil Brothers, your main goal should be getting your education because that is your main job and education is the key to success. Believe me I know it isn't easy going to school and staying focused on the prize because your mind is in so many different directions, but you must stay the course. Make a difference in your community.

Oh believe me, I truly understand that peer pressure is real because I remember watching my young brother when he was your age and it was very difficult. It was so difficult watching him that sometimes I would hear him telling my older brother about some of the things he was dealing with and I would hear my older brother telling my young brother that you have to stand your ground no matter what because if you don't people will continue bother you. The good thing about his situations he had several big brothers he could go to for advice so I say to you if you don't have any big brothers find yourself a male mentor or role model to help you get through your difficult times.

I understand that is a time in your life when you are easily impressed, but you have to stand your ground and stay firm in what you believe. Remember you are your biggest supporter. When you lose focus of the prize do you think your peers will care? No, they won't. Half of them don't really like you anyway. So it's up to you to care about yourself.

- Have confidence

- Self-respect

- Work hard on your academics

- Be active in your communities

- Reach out to help someone in need of your assistance.

"Set goals and accomplish them."
--Thomas—

<u>Hanging Out With The Wrong Crowd</u>

This relates to people of all genders and ages from early school to our professional careers. One of the most powerful forces of nature is an intangible object called influence. We often find ourselves wanting to be a part of something external to ourselves like a particular group of people. We sometimes want acceptance so badly we ignore our own core beliefs, values, and even morality and do not evaluate if the groups behavior or culture are aligned with our own.

For males who are often viewed with responsibility of being heads of household this is very troubling in our society as it shows a breakdown or absence of self-discipline.

It is true that right and wrong are both matters of perception but in every society there are standards that we must conform to in order to align with that existing culture.

When we choose to do things illegal outside of that alignment we are making a choice

To ignore the principals of social conformity and become a menace or non compliant to those set standards "a criminal" I am not stating that you should follow blindly everything that is considered policy but only to examine the course of consequences you may have to endure based on how you choose to protest.

<u>We Were Once Your Age</u>

I know at this age, you may think you are worn out from your parents making this statement. I can surely relate to that having been lectured myself consistently as a child.

The truth is that the world is the world and the situations that happen to people in every day life is trans generational. The elder people try to teach the young especially their children by sharing some of their life experiences. They have unpleasant experiences that may have been controlled or even avoided at times and want to share that so others do not make the same mistakes causing despair in their lives. We tend to call this sharing wisdom because often you cannot find it in a book because it is a life experience.

We will all have road maps to our lives sometimes getting lost along the way. The younger generation should consider wisdom as a type of GPS. It may not always guide you to the right place but when applied properly it will prevent you from taking a wrong turn in your life and off the road of pursuing happiness.

There are no problems only situations waiting to be corrected.

--Mark Mason--

<u>Devil's Playground</u>

An idle mind is the devil's playground.

—Unknown—

- Get involved in extracurricular activities.

- Seek Mentors

- Listen to motivational speaking CDs regularly to train your mind.

- Get a part-time job.

"Lil Brothers, whatever you do never give your power to anyone."

—Laura Simmons—
Author/Motivational Speaker

<u>Lil Brothers</u>

Don't allow people to mess you over; know your worth and stay focused. You have greatness within you! You can change your own life right now. Just remember you were born a KING and a KING leads he doesn't follow. Don't ever let anyone tell you anything different. Know you have so much to look forward to.

"Never quit! Always finish what you start."
--Dan--

<u>Stay On Top Of Your Game</u>

There are going to be many challenges that you will have to face. There isn't a book or a map to show you the correct path, but if you know what you want out of life you are your own map and the direction you are seeking for yourself is within you. Remember to stay the course if you want something out of this big world because it's not going to be easy.

(Keep this in mind; you work hard in the early part of your life, so as you get older

It gets better.) You can be anything if you put your mind to it.

Lil Brothers, always put your best foot forward and never doubt yourself. You don't have to be great to get started; you just have to get started to be great. When you feel you can't do it, grab yourself by the bootstrap and say I know I can do it. Go for the things that you want and don't let anything or anyone stop you, give it all you got, because no one is going to give you anything.

"To greatly increase your odds of success simply do what you're supposed to do when you're suppose to do it."
--Kevin Jackson—

<u>Life</u>

Life is very challenging, but you must stay the course no matter what the situation is because it is very rewarding.

"Don't waste time. Have a plan on how to become successful in life."
—Robert Harris—

<u>Choosing Your Friends</u>

It's good to be choosy of the people you call your friends or homies, Lil Brothers.

 Always keep this in mind:

- Just because you can doesn't mean you should

- Great minds discuss business (real talk)

- Average minds discuss events

- Poor minds discuss people

- It is very important to have strong self-esteem and confidence in yourself

- Faith in the most high is truly important.

- Stay true to yourself and the rest will fall in place

- Be careful of the company that you keep

- It's important to be sure of the crowd you find yourself in.

Set goals in life for yourself. Develop the self-discipline to stay the course and overcome your obstacles.
—David Simmons—

<u>Meaningful Relationships</u>

Know your worth Lil Brothers. You are worthy of a meaningful relationship with a good person. Don't settle because you think there are no other options. Relationships like that usually become violent relationships. You are worthy of a healthy and meaningful relationship.

"Hitting a woman doesn't make you a man."
—Brandon—

Time With Self

Lil Brothers, take time for you. Remember, the best way to learn what makes you happy or sad is time spent with yourself.

"You have a choice in life choose wisely."
—Author/Motivational Speaker Laura Simmons—

<u>Your Destiny</u>

Lil Brothers, your destiny is to be great so don't let anyone steal that from you!

"When you fail that means you're one step closer to success so keep going."
—Ramonn—
<u>Rapper/Actor/Author</u>

<u>Choices In Life</u>

Always keep this in mind, Lil Brothers; just because you can doesn't mean you should. The choices you make determine the life you will have. Let me tell you, there isn't a map on the correct path to take to be successful because to become successful means that there will be bumps in the road. It's what you do when you run into them bumps that determine the life you will have. In short, choose wisely on the choices you make for your life.

'Always ask questions, be a good listener surround yourself with quality people, listen to the voice of experience and always treat people the way you want to be treated."
—Tim Grant—

<u>Help Another Brother</u>

Always try to help each other; if your brother needs a helping hand help him. Let's also do better with not always throwing shade at each other because it is not easy for any of you. Life is a very complicated puzzle and usually it is easier to figure it out if you surround yourself with positive resources, friends, and of course family.

That's why it is important to lend a helping hand. You are your brother's keeper!

"No matter what you are dealing with trust in God and be a blessing to others regardless of what the situation may be. Try to be all that you want to be in life because we only get one chance."

--Jermaine Moses—
Businessman

I Still Have Faith

"I still have faith in my Lil Brothers. Now let's make this world a better place for the Lil Brothers that are coming behind you! Spread your positive knowledge. It's a brotherhood that you must carry on to the next generation. You must empower all the Lil Brothers you know and reach out to the ones you don't know.

Help them to first understand and then focus on the bigger picture. "

"Stay focused the future is yours to shape!!"
—David Simmons—

Putting The Hard Work In Now

- Sometimes taking the easy way can make your life harder then it has been.

- Retire young and see the world.

- Reboot yourself when you feel unsuccessful, but giving up is not the answer.

- Surround yourself with winners. Live the dream; become creative it's in you.

- Find your purpose and go after it.

- Nothing comes to a dreamer but dreams. So stop dreaming about it and do something about it.

- Make it happen.

Thoughts Of Suicide

It is important to talk to your parents or a family member that you are close to because they cannot read your mind. We know that you may be dealing with some very difficult situations, but taking your life is never the answer. Do you realize how many people you will hurt with your actions?

Truly think about all the people you are hurting. Think about the people that truly love you and think about what happens to your soul when you take your life.

I know you may probably feel like your parents don't understand, or they will judge you. Let me tell you something; give them a try because your parents have not always been adults. They have been down these roads more times than you can imagine.

Who is the best teacher? Someone who has already been through the things you are going through. Guess what? That will be your parents or grandparents! No, they are not your friends; they are your parents and truly love you no matter what!

Okay, I think some of you may be saying, "I don't even have a relationship with my parents." Well, I know there are grandparents, uncles, aunts, teachers, doctors, nurses, pastors or even the lady behind the counter at your favorite store. Please reach out to someone preferably someone that is responsible enough to help you through your tough times.

The suicide hotline number is 1-800-273-8255 and it is available 24 hours a day.

"Build as many positive relationships as possible and cherish them."
—David—

<u>Just Don't Give Up</u>

"Keep this in mind-doubt kills more dreams than failure ever will."
--Genius mindset—

Remember the cemetery is the richest place, why? Because there are some many people that had big dreams but never went after their dreams so their dreams died with them. So put your dreams to work now because it does no good there in the cemetery.

Don't be afraid to take a chance. Where there is one NO there's a YES waiting around the corner. Just don't give up.

<u>Peer Pressure</u>

Lil Brothers, you are going to face all kinds of peer pressure. This is why you must be confident in the person you are becoming. You will frequently encounter situations where people are going to try to persuade you to do things. It is important that you listen to your gut. Your gut is your stomach; it's going to let you know when things are not right. For example, your friend is going to go into a store and try to steal something. Your gut is going to feel nervous. Lil Brothers, listen to that feeling. That is your spirit telling you that you shouldn't go into the store with him you should go home. Follow that feeling.

Lil Brothers you are all unique individuals that have the power to be great individuals. Do not allow your peers to pressure you to do anything that is against the definition of you.

Lil Brothers, remember you are a lion. That means you are a king and ruler of the jungle. Will you face pressure in life? Of course you will that's why it is important to stay focused and follow your dreams. When life's roads take a curve, you take a pause and that means its time to hit the reset button to move forward.

"Don't waste time have a plan on how to become successful in life."
—Robert Harris—

<u>Dressing To Impress</u>

Lil Brothers, be aware of your appearance. I'm not saying you have to put on dress slacks and dress shoes everyday, but sometimes it is good to switch it up.

Lil Brothers, you can be cool without sagging them pants because I'm sure some of you don't know that this was a fashion born of a prison mode of signaling sexual availability.

Let's put positivity back into what our young men should look like. Remember Lil Brothers; you are representing the kings that came before you. Lets make them proud.

Let's work more on how we present ourselves to the world. Lil Brothers lets motivate, inspire, encourage and develop self-esteem within us so that you can pass it on to the lil kings that are watching you.

<u>Lil Brothers, Hear Me Out! Reboot Yourself!</u>

~ 36 ~

"Stay true to yourself and be your own man."
—Horace Smith—

There Is A Big World Out There To See

Lil Brothers, **HUSTLE LEGALLY!** You are not too young to start thinking about seeing the world. There are so many places to see outside your neighborhood. Start saving that allowance money or sell items you don't wear or use anymore, on one of these online stores such as old shoes, clothes, book bags, jackets etc. You get my point. Now they have there are so many legal ways to make money to save for that summer vacation.

Lil Brothers, make it your business to learn a second language. Get out and enjoy life, take an acting class or cooking class learn something besides football and basketball. Lil Brothers, try learning as much as you can while you are young. I'm not saying you can't learn when you get older, but why waste time; the time is now.

I think of all the great opportunities that are out here for us now and we don't take advantage of it because we are trying to keep an eye on the wrong things. Get out there and live!!!

Communication Skills

Lil Brothers it is important to develop your communication skills…

When someone says "hello" to you, acknowledge him or her with a "hello" back. Do not wave or not say anything, as that is just straight rude! Speak when spoken to.

When you talk to people look them straight in the eyes. It shows that you are truly paying attention to them and that you are being truthful in your conversation with them. Making eye contact with people tells a lot about you as a person. Communication happens with your eyes while you're listening just as much as when you are talking. Also, remember to give them a smile.

Communication skills help you in college and in the work force. Knowing how to communicate is an asset that can take you very far in life.

Take responsibility for the things you can do now to prepare yourself for your bright future. You hold the keys to every aspect of your life.

<u>Working On The Creative Side Of You</u>

There will be powers within you that you didn't even know existed. You have to be in touch with yourself to know your powers and what you can do. Use that creative side of you to grow into the young men you are meant to be. Maybe there is something well that you can do, like cut hair, communicate with people, fix cars, play basketball, speak in front of large crowds, shop for clothes, debate, sing or dance. Whatever it may be, it's within you. Let it shine. Let the world see you are a gift.

You were born to create paths not follow them you can do this! You are going to make it once you discover your creative side, and then there's no stopping you.

"My mom always used to say to me that I was the most headstrong of her children. That's only because I knew I wanted so much out of life, but I wasn't sure how to get to it. I was the youngest, but I always had big dreams, big goals, and big desires.

I used my creative side to attract things I wanted in life."

–Author/Motivational Speaker Laura Simmons—

<u>Vision</u>

Where do you see yourself 10 years from today?

Speak volumes into your life meaning speak what you want to see yourself doing in 10 years and started preparing yourself to get there; Start by surrounding yourself with like-minded people that can help you reach your goals. You heard the saying; you lay down with dogs you will catch fleas!

Well take that to heart because if you hang out with broke fools you will be one of those broke fools. You have to plant seeds so you can get the harvest you are seeking. You have to have a vision. You have to be committed to your vision.

I strongly believe life is setup for us to succeed, but we have to give it all we have to get there. You must not give up on your vision no matter what your dealt. You must stay the course there will be bumps in the road and you may fall a couple of times on the way, but remember if you can look up you can definitely get up and get back into the game.

"Never quit always finish what you start."
--Dan--

Random Thoughts

- You can't fail at being your own man.

- Never let behaviors of others destroy your inner peace.

- Big dreams have to be conquered in stages; don't try to accomplish them all at once.

- Stay true to yourself and be your own man.

- Follow your dreams.

- Never let anyone tell you that you can't because you can do anything you set your mind to do you were born a king.

- Love that person you see in the mirror more then anyone else even when it seem like no one else does.

- Watch the crowd you keep because some crowds aren't good for you.

- Known that you have a choice in life choose wisely.

- Always ask questions when you aren't sure.

- Never let anger drive your actions.

(Set goals and accomplish each and every one of them)

Having Mentors

Having mentors are very important and to me there is no particular age that you should be to have them. Hell I have plenty of mentors, male and female because you can learn a lot from them. Mentors provide personal support to help you succeed. Having mentors can help enhance you and make your chances of succeeding greater.

The benefit of having mentors in your life:

They can help you improve your communication skills.

They can help establish positive and trusting relationships.

They can help you expand your horizons.

They can help you with self-reflection and so much more….

Failure is success in progress!

A few of My Mentors

Handling Bullying

Steps to Handling Bullying Situations:

Lil Brothers, if you are being bullied, please tell an adult it's not snitching! I know that's what you young people call it today. The adult will listen to you and then talk with the bullies but they will make sure you are safe.

When faced with a bullying situation, please try to stay calm. Do not allow the bully to control your actions.

Lil Brothers, bullies are dealing with low self-esteem and insecurities. I know this will be hard, but try to be your bullies' friend. Nine times out of ten someone at home is bullying this person and they are taking their anger out on you just because they can. Remember what I told you early on; just because you can doesn't mean you should.

Protect yourself also from the cyber-bullying; please be aware of your actions on social media. Lil-Brothers, if you are a victim of cyber bullying, please block and delete that person from your friends' list and make sure you report it to an adult. If the person attends your school, please tell an adult right away!

Lil Brothers, if you notice someone being bullied, reach out and be a friend. Bullying is a serious situation so I strongly encourage you to tell a responsible adult.

<u>Relationships</u>

I don't claim to know everything, Lil Brothers, but what I do know about relationships is that it is important to be in a healthy relationship. A young lady should not hit on you and you should definitely never put your hands on a young lady. I know how you young people like to play the hitting games that end up into a domestic violence situation.

The best way to avoid that is to not to start it. Studies show that nearly 1.5 million high school students nationwide experience physical abuse from dating a partner in a single year. One in 10 high school students has been purposely hit, slapped or physically hurt by a boyfriend or girlfriend.

Remember you must have self-care. If you have questions about your relationship or think you may be in an unhealthy relationship please reach out for help. If you see a friend of yours in a violently domestic situation, reach out to them and get them some help by letting an adult know.

"Hitting a young doesn't make you a man."
—Brandon—

<u>Information For Help</u>

National Suicide Prevention Lifeline:

1-800-273-8255

National Runaway Safe line:

1-800-RUNAWAY

Domestic Violence Hotline:

1-800-799-7233 or TTY

1-800-787-3224

STD Information and referrals to STD Clinics:

1-800-232-6348

Drug/ Alcohol Rehab:

1-866-684-6303

Mental Health Assistance:

1-888-844-6026

Mental Health Treatment Free Help:

1-877-819-2152

<u>A Prayer For Everyone</u>

Dear Heavenly Father,

I come to you just as I am, not for fame or fortune. I come to you to ask that you wrap your loving arms around all my Lil Brothers. I ask that you guide their steps and protect them from harm and danger each and everyday. Oh Lord some of our young men need more guidance and directions than others, but either way I come to you to cover and bless them in every step of their lives.

I ask that you heal those that need healing and for those that need a change in their lives, I ask that you grant it to them. I ask that you strengthen those that need strengthening and I ask that you keep them in their right mind and for those that are not, I ask that you keep them and keep giving them strength.

Lord, I ask that you protect them from their bullies and the peer pressure that they may be dealing with right now.

In the name of the almighty, I say Amen!

<u>Growing Up In The Hood</u>

I'm not telling you guys this story for guilt, or to shame the community I grew up in. I am telling you this story in motivation to seek the highest achievements that life has to offer you, and to not settle for minimal perceptions of you as black men. When I was 14 years old, I was profiled on my way to the barbershop. Most people would say, "well that's an everyday situation for me". Unfortunately, that is the reality of what I lived. I simply walked out of my home and saw an undercover cop car driving out of my alleyway. They stopped and stared at me as if I was a criminal. I had a hoodie over my head and locked the house for them to see I had keys. Somehow, as I walked down the street the drove onto the curb and blocked me in from continuing to walk. They hemmed me to the fence and questioned me about why I was at the house. Long story short, they assumed I was like my environment trying to be up to no good. As black boys and black men we must carry ourselves with respect, or we will continue to be profiled and mistreated. Now I am 26 years old and I know my perception of the law isn't the best, but I appreciate that situation I had because it was for the protection of the property, I stayed in. My note to you guys is to self-reflect on your character. Understand who you are, and who you are becoming to others. If it creates more conflict, then make an adjustment and you'll see the payoff.

Be Blessed,

Dana

<u>Safety Tips When Driving And You Get Pulled Over</u>

1. Turn your vehicle off

2. Make sure you put your ID on the dashboard before the police comes up to your vehicle

3. Make sure radio volume is down low

4. Both hands on the steering wheel with all fingers up

5. When they ask you for your ID, make sure you tell them you are reaching for your ID, which should be on the dashboard.

6. Do not argue with the officer

7. Make sure you address them as "Officer"

PLEASE STAY SAFE!!

"Obey your parents, fear God and serve him.
--Prophet Green--

<u>Thanking Everyone</u>

I want to shout out a few of my teachers before I move on to the people that have supported my dreams from day one.

First, I want to thank my Ma, Ceta (My Mom), who is no longer with me in the physical, but always by my side spiritually. That is my mother Margaret Harris. Mama taught me so much and believe me when I say it was not easy Growing up I thought I knew more than she did, so I know for fact it wasn't easy raising me. However, I thank my mom for instilling in me all that she could because it made me a better person.

I want to think my dad. He was the first King I knew, Thomas Harris Sr., who is also always by my side spiritually. Dad taught me so such about the Male species. I could remember my dad was the hardest working man I knew, even with the odds being against him. He taught me how to hustle and get what I wanted out of life and I thank you Dad!!

I want to thank all my sisters and brothers for all the lessons about life that have been taught to me over the years; from learning how to ride a bike, to learning how to fight for my rights.

I want to thank my husband (David) for telling me I can do anything I set my mind to.

He always tells me how proud he is of what I have accomplished.

I want to thank my two beautiful children, Rashad and Roshonda. You talking about two people that are always rooting for me and telling me how proud they are of me, these two would win the award.

I would like to thank all our supporters of The Mother Daughter Team LLC!!

A Note To Margaret Greene

Margaret Greene:

When I say thank you, I mean it from the bottom of my heart. You are my big sister, my mentor and my friend who I know for a fact that will always have my back. You have been my prayer warrior, a huge part of my support system, and I thank you. I thank you for your inspiration in helping me to be the best that I can be. I thank you for the many conversations we had when I wanted to give up. I remember when we were younger I was always taller than you, but I knew you were still the big sister because when I would cry you would always be there to tell me everything would be okay.

Thank you sister for your love and support!!

Love, your baby sister,

Laura

A Note To Sophia Woods-Simmons

My sister & my friend. I thank you for you being the little sister I always wanted.

When I say I thank you for all that you do I truly mean it from the bottom of my heart. You are my support system, my friend, my exercise coach and my mentor, and I just want to say thanks. I thank you for your inspiration in helping me excel and grow in my quest for success. Thank you sister/friend for your love and support!

Love you,

Laura

<u>Jean Harris</u>

This book is for you Sissy! R. I. P.

I lost my biggest supporter but I gained another angel!

You are truly missed.

Love, your baby Sissy,

Laura

A Note To All The Lil Brothers (From Charlie)

I wasn't born a prisoner, so I ask you Lil Brothers to listen up!

I have served 18 years so far and I still try to keep my faith and believe I will someday soon be able to walk out of this place. You see I was sentenced to life in jail and I say to you this hasn't been a picnic. I lost my mom, my favorite aunt and two of my sisters since I've been locked up in this place.

I didn't get to see my children grow up and now I have grandchildren whom I desperately would like to meet and do all the things a grandfather does with his grandchildren, but because of my hard head and my stubbornness.

I am in a place where I really don't belong. I got mixed up with the wrong crowd of people and they are free while I'm locked up. I'm not mad at them. I'm mad at myself because I had crazy skills, but I chose a different path that I knew wasn't right and I let my anger drive my actions. You see it's the choices we make that put us in situations like this because if I had kept my record clean in the first place it wouldn't have been easy for them to frame me for things I am serving time for now.

If there is one thing I could hear my mother saying to me it would be this; "It's easy as hell to get in trouble, but it's hard as hell to get out." BOY OH BOY! How true that was! You see there is no reason why I should be here because I had every opportunity that my siblings had--we had both our parents living under the same roof and they loved each and every one of us. I had big brothers that for every birthday whatever I said I wanted they made a way for me to get it and they always had my back no matter what I was supposed to set an example for my younger siblings, but because I thought I knew it all I'm here serving life in a place I shouldn't be.

You ask why I'm telling you this; my prayer is that you take notes so you can make better choices and surround yourself with better friends than what I had and I don't blame anyone but myself. Lil Brothers, listen to that little voice deep inside you that will give you crazy pangs when something isn't right. Remember no one can help you unless you help yourself. I hope what I told you will help you make better decisions then I did. Now get out there and live life and see the world Lil Brothers. You have a choice in life, choose wisely.

Love Big Brother,

Chuck

<u>The War</u>

Young men the storm has just begun It isn't over.

There is so much more rain heading your way. Young men, wake up! You have to survive in order for our people to grow and keep getting stronger. There is a war out here. We must become stronger for our nation. Mentally and physically, we are not ready. Lil Brothers, Pull the pants up and shake someone's hand. You are young Kings! Lil Brothers, just hear me out!!

Author/ Motivational Speaker

Laura

LIL BROTHERS, HEAR ME OUT
Author Laura Simmons

NOTES

<u>NOTES</u>

~ 71 ~

<u>NOTES</u>

~ 72 ~

<u>NOTES</u>

~ 73 ~

www.ingramcontent.com/pod-product-compliance
Lightning Source LLC
Chambersburg PA
CBHW051007060726
47593CB00017B/1106